He Is Walking Wider

He Is Walking Wider

Poems by

Ellen Pober Rittberg

Cover design by Shay Culligan

ISBN: 978-1-954353-72-5

Kelsay Books
502 South 1040 East, A-119
American Fork, Utah, 84003

This book is dedicated to the memory of my parents, Pearl and Nathan Pober and my children and grandchildren.

Acknowledgments

The author is grateful to the editors of the following publications where these poems first appeared:

CW Post College Annual Community Poetry Journal: "Impel"
Cobra Milk: "San Miguel de Allende"
First Literary Review East: "Spring"
Flutter: "He Is Walking Wider"
Great Weather for Media 2019 Anthology: "What I Think About When I Think About My Morning Commute"
Griffel Literary Magazine: "Leavetaking, a Guide," "Lissa"
Long Island Quarterly: "Childhood's Cusp"
Persian Sugar in English Tea, a bilingual anthology, vol. 1: "Forest," "Song of the City," "Remembering Max Wheat, Nature Walk"
PoetryBay: "Mom," "On Mom's Yahrzeit, the Second Anniversary of her Death"
Polarity: "In Celebration of Brooklyn" (appeared under the title, "Paean to Whitman II, 2019")
Raintiger: "Matthew, Age 12," "Dad"
sn Review: "They Follow Her," "Funny How the Heart"
Sensitive Skin: "Dig"
Slow Trains: "See Her Hands How They Plait"

Contents

He Is Walking Wider

He is walking wider and wider arcs
have you seen him,
my son, the biggest one
striding, alone,
on the highway overpass
straddling the horizon
above heaving trucks,
the world passing furiously?

He marks his way steadily
across our broad town
an ocean wave at low tide.
He watches the geese on their course,
the merchants closing their stores.
Perhaps he wonders where he fits.

He journeys far.

Still, I must let him
and when darkness spills
on the Malaga-wine sky
and he returns home,
I must enjoy his levelness
and his curls
wending down his neck,
goats down a mountain.
I must praise him
and remember to pat
his manly shoulders.
This child will cut through the world,
will make smooth sharp grooves
and sometimes may even lead me.

They Follow Her

they follow her
with their eyes
ready to attach
themselves to her
they come ashore
she shakes off
her composure
like sleep
and they are
fooled by it.
she breaks
herself off
in pieces
like taffy,
the sea enters her
the men advance on her

for centuries
she sits
at her islet
with no outlet
a small Hellenic
trade-route post
she sees all
she lives alone
and those who come to call
are consumed
by her lizard eye glance
her berry red hellion craw.

I like the woman's power
I like her pluck.

Forest

Carolina wren I beg you
Show yourself
Your liquid pure sound
From highest arch
Has song ever been this clear
This sound discernment-judgement
Not like the mockingbird
Tail high prone to pronouncement
Why imitate at all
When your repertoire
Is so varied
Piano player in large hotel.
There's a special place in my heart
For fungus
Spectral white or buttercup yellow scalloped
      capped or cupped
And clouds that hover
Devoid of omen
And rocks ragged jagged
Some composite
Once pyroclastic
Waldeinsamkeit
My natural juice
My equipoise

See Her Hands How They Plait

see her hands how they plait
beneath her head as she sleeps
she works upon it
like some field
that might yield ripe red grapes
if she works hard enough
which she always does.
see her arms as she reaches out
steadily upon her bed cloths
always going
she wants so much, this child
the raw force impels her up
impels her to the sun.
sometimes she grabs at me
as if I am some tattered cloth,
grabs at my shoulder
my thigh, with great force,
like some mythic creature
she cannot be shaken off.
do not give her a life
of vague longings
watching the world
from room corners
her body, bowed
but let her not run too fast
into a window
as she once did,
the scar
on her forehead
a square
which she displays
proudly
her diadem.

let the world rise
when she enters the room
absorb her
but not fully—
pulsate with her
watch her emerge, converge
not to blend or efface,
but to brace
the world with her hand
band it like a bird
give voice to it
without singing
to stand, withstand
love, be beloved
to trace the world
with her finger
and tread upon it
enter it
as if for the first time
with grace
elemental
a fantast
walking into the wind
a singer in the dark
as tall as the Eastern Pine
as ancient.

Song of the City

Awash in ginkgo leaves on street
Fans discarded others brittle curled turning in
human life at terminus and knowing it
receding
I photograph my shoe perpetual motion
Man as whirligig but smooth, man the purveyor
I buy life I sell it
To myself mostly
sunrise's umbilicus obscured by objects urban
seen as nectarine band splayed across horizon
Uncooked omelette
I perceive them all:
doorways sidewalk art
One says 'protect yo heart' and I do
I gird it unburthen it rarely and to few
Oh, the solitary life is a lovely life
is a lonely life is a riff on melody
A roundelay of song
And ah and so
I sing it lustily long

Childhood's Cusp

Axl Rose' falsetto plays
as my three kids,
combs, hair gel in hand
vie for space
around narrow corridor mirror
amped up versions of themselves
readying for middle school dance.
"Get out of my room,"
oldest child says to youngest,
voice lower than I remember.

Now grown into less amusing
but equally lovable adults,
they roar with laughter
watching video of that night,
speech no longer
heavily inflected,
less like me now
complete iterations
grace notes
attuned to the greater world.

Now closer,
never harsh with each other,
they do not laugh as much.
Nor do they think
of time's passage,
its signal moments,
instead reveling in
what they have come to see
as love refined, burnished,
these tight sheaves
healthy wheat.

In Celebration of Brooklyn

for Walt Whitman

1.

Particulate particular
to us all
the cleaving to and clasping of
arms, hair, thighs, to connect,
intersect, to feel
dew between toes,
you on the grass
me on dead tree now turned to
soil
like us, rich with possibility,
or standing in Prospect Park
on tree roots
folding going up
leading to the heavens:
Jack's beanstalk.
Where do we go together
or alone communing in dark
or in dank subway tunnels,
the workers worming down canals?
Shall we sing huzzahs for them?
We shall.

2.

Speaking Polish
round older man and woman
close metal storefront
with a clunk
worn but not defeated.

3.

I too am older
but native born and
hopeful in the way
those who live in words
and ochre paint
who troll parks
and chitter with birds are.

4.

New Brooklyn:
men in porkpie hats
women in diaphanous skirts
writers and readers in cafes
facing out open doors, windows,
and everywhere,
discourse.
Art and clothing
hang in stores
concatenations,
Rauschenberg-inspired,
a gloss on the consumer text.
Similarly inspired,
I resolve to make
art from repurposed panty hose
or remember:

5.

myself, age six,
my sandwich
to be eaten
when I came home
from school
for lunch,
or of a dime,
wax paper wrapped,
rubber banded
thrown to me by Mother
from apartment window
the price of truck-mounted ride
parked curbside, The Whip
which whirred our bodies hither
and yon.

6.

Maybe the lilt
of the speech
of the hospital worker
from Haiti, Jamaica. Nevis,
St. Lucia, Barbados, Trinidad
& islands, mostly Caribbean,
is the sound of the sea
as it floats to the shore
to make haste
to make life
stir it up
crustaceans burbling
seaweed swilling.

I hear them, their voices
in hospital corridors
the just-folks
some newly arrived
others not—
all of them
making cities thrum.
Some sing
as they mop and swish swish and mop
or hum lute-like.
Such hope!
Such piquancy of speech
like their countries' birds
the scarlet ibis, the
crested caracara
the flame orange troupial,
some, with wingspans fantastical
larger than Mardi Gras floats.
But here, abide the
crows who cavort cavil
and grackles
whose song is a creaking door.

7.

Awash in dreams
in Brooklyn
we are a nation undivulged.
I take its paths.
I run like Diana.
Looping darting,

a barn swallow flies
alongside East River
alongside Brooklyn Bridge Park dock
past shock of purple paulownia
and yet,
it is still morning!

San Miguel De Allende, 1969

Below towering church,
all gilt all ornament,
the old woman selling seeds
in cones
of newspaper
squats.
It's morning.

I'm eating my morning roll,
sugared up,
baked goods, the only kind of food
I'll eat.
I drink only boiled water
and Coca Cola in glass bottles.
I become thin, gaunt almost,
but healthily so.

A trumpet sounds.
Mariachis, costumed festooned,
march down sharp curves and alleys.
The trumpeter leads,
his notes *pizzicato.*

The shoemaker crafts me
custom boots too small.
I won't discover this
until I'm home in the States.

A man walks on the moon.
We all huddle watching.
The small step remains
a small step.

The following year
the public turns against
space exploration
thinks the cost is too high.
A far more costly war blazes
in Vietnamese forests.
We learn a new word: napalm.

I'm developing a crush
on a bullfighter, Jaime,
only he doesn't like me
although he doesn't know me.
He throws me into his pool
with too much force.
Is it because I'm Jewish?
There are no Jews here
or none that announce it.

Years later, I watch a bullfight
in Cancun.
The matador can't seem to
kill the bull.
A shit show.
The bull lived or
at least I think he did.

In a bar, the ex-pats expound upon
what ex-pats expound upon.
It rains every day at four
reliable as rain, I should say
or think.
But I am only there for a summer so
its impact I think is minimal.

I thought about that rain,
that summer recently,
why, I'm not quite certain.
Wrote a poem about it.
Not this one.

Florida, Visiting My Sister

A cloud moves.
It is so close
I try to catch it.
It is as remote
as my mother was
to all others.
Sun overtakes the cloud.

My staple food as a baby,
doctor's orders:
skimmed milk boiled three times
and cottage cheese and bananas.
I ask my sister if she remembers
she slipped me raisins—or so
Mom told it.
She doesn't.

I cried when photographed,
a nervous child,
still am.

I thought bullfrogs
at my sister's condo
in man-made pond
were fans whirring.
Silly me.

Snowy egret skulks, stops
crimp-necked, crest feather
askew
his patience medieval.
He needs a comb.

We visit a Gilded Age mansion.
Rain falls on copper-clad roof
Bing. Louder. Bing bing bing,
a cash register,
old school.

A patch of my garden spigot
rust-orange hair
turns forge red of its own accord.
Refusing to turn white or
gray, my hair defies time,
others' expectations
which I regard as a gift
or a symbol of sorts.

Online Dating, 2019

My daughter paid,
says I'm lonely.
I post myself in jersey dress
clingy even with a slip.
Sans jewelry sans excess anything.
I am the image of moderation.

I swipe left all men whose flash
        bounces
                      off
              mirrors.
While selfie-taking skill
is not *de rigueur,* knowing
someone, anyone, well enough,
to take their picture, is.

I swipe left men who
            say they served time
 swiping faster past men who look as if they did.

I double-swipe the man who gushes
his soulmate will be "someone
who likes to eat at midnight."

I write to a man
whose face pressed against his dog's
looks like Cerberus.
I get no response, which
depresses me. This depression
depresses me.

"You look like you work out,"
one man writes.
I demur from writing back.

To the man who writes
he "doesn't like women
who play games"
I refrain from replying:
You mean, Monopoly?"

I mull over a name change
from Natural Woman to
Finely Honed and Ironic
or I Only Look Dour.
Instead, I google
the correct pronunciation of dour.

I rule out posting
a cheesecake photo
me in a bathing suit at water's edge,
slight lunge suggesting
I am part gym rat
part Botticelli's Venus.

App sends men
whose "paths I cross"
which should creep me out
but doesn't.

I linger on the man who boasts he
reads only professional journals.
Narrow though his reading choices may be,
he may pick up the tab
unlike the man I thought
I was meeting for coffee
and not a pricey five course
non-prix-fixed meal
whose recitation of his employment history

caused my head to dip
precipitously close to my *vichyssoise.*

I cast my geographic net wider
"Sorry there's a bridge
between us," says New Jersey Bob.
to New York Ellen.
Riiiiiight.

Not ready to pack it in—
I delete men who don't know
the difference between it's and its.

Can I lie and say I'm active
because they say they're active?
Shall I say there's a fine line between
facial hair and Unabomber hair
or say, Let me introduce you to a
kindergartner's best friend, the comb?

As to the man who asked me,
"tell me your philosophy of kissing"
I'm glad, so glad, at that moment
my cell phone died.

Funny How the Heart

funny how the heart heaves
and in one convulsive sigh
dies.

does it wear out
or did it will itself
to stop,
ending
disconnected days
in clubs
playing cards with men
you did not know
paying as you went,
your absence never noted,
sitting amid impatient women
who pointed out the imperfections
of your game.

funny how the frame looks gaunt
and stops when the pounds slip off,
less work to pump, or so it would seem
but the heart works fitfully
works hard
and for what?
you must have asked yourself
more than once
until the thought became a chant
a hum:
and you must have heard the wind reply:
"no purpose. none."

funny how the earth spins on,
leaving the unwary soul to
grasp,
to hurl oneself upon the globe
and then to open up the palm.

Father, Dad, Pop, you must have known
that you must cinch the world
like a too-tight belt
and grab on
and squeeze your eyelids
even while you sleep
to survive,
you knew because
you embraced the world
a chaste lover without a motive.
I fear chasms with peaks inside
pitched high,
but you would have wanted me
to hold on
as you would have held on
had you remembered.

oh, some lapses
life makes no allowances for
I must remember
I must remember that.

Remembering Max Wheat, Nature Walk

sparrow robin
all song
red-winged blackbird
rash percussive
a street band
ring necked pheasant
tail long string of
a wind-up toy:
floating, milkweed

I like the Russian olive tree
open penetrating my nostrils
becoming my lungs
but I like it better closed
pendulous
each bud a promise
my own invention.

tree swallow overhead
close enough to touch
"a flicker of sardine light,"
I say observe
"that's a poet thinking,"
Max says
his name eponymous with
at-one-with nature: wheat.
"write it down,"
he commands.
and I do, have been walking
with Max a generation now
at Bryant's home Cedarmere
fall maple leaves
lighting up the sky

hiking Whitman's path
on Long Island Jayne's Hill
and today amid cypress spurge
bird's-foot violet
upon denuded land, century-old wagon rut
we walk our Long Island
terminal moraine
outwash
and nowhere are we far from water
fine ocean sand the color of
some primitive goddess' top-knotted hair
the pocked white stones of the Sound
the color of Zeus' temple some colonnade
on this the very last prairie
east of the Mississippi
I pet the grass last year's
now soft etiolated soft as puppy's fur.
see shards of ancient columns

I must go must resolve to walk again where Whitman walked.
Adieu!

What I Think About When I Think About My Morning Commute

When we fight sleep do we fight death
The
The un-aspired to
The thing in the closet
That may be alive
That isn't meant

And we know it
On some level we know it
The dust ball
From disused sweater
A tatter of plastic seen
Seemingly teeming
Organic

Comedic almost antic,
That that great fooler
Adrenalin thumper
The choice prime steak
Runny pink
I never eat but once did
Okay maybe thrice
Don't think of that either
Not because of any
Widely held beliefs

The broad berth
Of my beliefs astonish
But just

Chewing I find arduous
Don't know why
My teeth are strong

Yellowish like a horse
Is she kidding
No
That was how
They judged health
in days of then or

Yore
Let us say yore
Yes let's
Great word
Got to get
Got to get the word in play
Acquisitive-like
Got to be in it
To win it
Thus spaked the New York
Lotter-ay
Aye as affirmation
What happened to that?

May I bray
I have the teeth for it
May I construct as Tinker Toy construction
As well constructed grammatical function
As in you will you say yes, yes
Don't ask
Shall we
Politesse

Do I belong here
In this here-here
In this eon
Mesozoic

Paleotropic
Never can keep them in order
Not that it matters
Still there's a
Critical mass

Dancing

Full of want
and wanting
to dance
she does.
Her moves are
jazz-infused, she
dances to her mind's
tone poem or
Joe Williams singing
*"Don't Get Around
Much Any More."*
Others' hips,
heads, hands
churn flail.
but not hers.
She sidles, slides,
her aimed-for image:
mellow subdued.

Young adulthood:
she meets, marries.
He insists they always be first
on the dance floor
thinks they cut an arresting figure
conjoined gyroscopes
holding hands amid
ocean of fellow dancers
who all dance to rock music
hands unclasped.

He tells her she is
the prettiest woman
in the room and
while in his arms

she believes it
in part because
there are not that many
women in the room.

He teaches her one and a half dances:
the *Paso Doble,*
which nobody dances to
and a basic swing sequence:
a curl and unfurl
his arm, snaking around hers,
and hers upon his,
then launches her
into a smart spin,
which he regards as
their couple thing
which she knows is
their only couple thing.

She used to love dancing
the merengue,
pre-him,
which he claims
he knows but when
she asks him
he refuses,
no reason given.

Through time
within his arms,
increasing mass,
she finds the cocoon feeling
lasts only as long
as the dance.

"Thrill is Gone" plays
in her head.
Mind tamps it down,
easier to—

Married and several years in,
he refuses to dance to anything.
When asked why, he shrugs.

Decades later
he will answer no questions
won't engage in the small acts of
daily living,
a Bartleby.
His mind, though not as such unhinged,
is a car in neutral
which she regards as
sad, tragic even.

Wiser now
and free,
she rarely feels
that pulsing foot-tapping need
but when it strikes, she lets loose
to piped music wherever she is,
dances at public functions
sometimes with,
sometimes without others
finding the life of a singleton
a thing of beauty
requiring no momentum
no arm-flings.

Mom

Days, your eyes clamped shut
nights you grab hard
a sailor hoisting rope,
nod as if to say "good"
teeth clap, castanets.

Synapses don't snap.
Dud fireworks.

Always spare, you
doled words out,
Tahitian pearls.

A motherless child,
you saw the world
through a dark prism,
silence your cocoon.

Your feet still cave-cold
under blanket heap.
Odd I didn't see cold feet
and your not being much
longer as one thing,
wanted to piece together
the shards but your body
marked time poorly.

Breath

Watergate gave us a scare,
I, we the people, watched.
Democracy prevailed.
So why am I thinking about Sonja Henie
in her hooded fur parka
1940s Norwegian Olympian-skater-
turned-Hollywood movie star
in *She's Working Her Way*
Through College
curls bobbing
blades spearing ice?
She lunched with Hitler,
saluted him.

Had I been there
I'd be bones, dust,
Zyklon Z entering my nose, lungs,
silent as cats.

I keep thinking about Trayvon Martin
whose life was robbed
extinguished
coming home to his Dad
his murder state-sanctioned
then ratified by a jury.

Shouldn't such wrongs
course through us?

Before cattle cars carried Jews
to extermination camps
Nazis used trucks, turned

exhaust pipes inward on Jews.
Is carbon dioxide death
silent?

Other murderous techniques
they used:
Jews were forced to dig
trenches to fall into
when shot dead,
bodies
upon
bodies. Heaps.

If Earth's recesses
crumbled,
our orbit wobbled
for each death
unpunished,
unrecorded,
would our planet
be peopled?

Spring

An enfilade of
flowers
march
down
mountain.
Petals nod in
affirmation,
wind-shook
but barely.
Perfect day.
Butterfly glides
diffident
touching down on flower
whose sex peers out
from bell shaped dress
a crinoline.

Matthew, Age 12

"Give me a kiss,"
I ask the kid
small, tough, compressed
Bessemer steel
green eyes
dark eyelashes
such a child has power
secrets
he denies it with a horse's whinny.

"What's in it for me," he answers
feinting
head cocked eyes narrowed
cheek soft and inviting
a newborn's.
he allows me my daily quota: one kiss, only one
I catch him fast and dry and on the wing.

sometimes, though
I don't even approach him
when he's lying
on the bed
hunched up
buried under wad of quilt covers.
I sit beside him, silent
feel his soles brush
against me
I am his mountain
and he is fierce and kittenish.

each day he goes outside
and plays in fields in cold breezes
staying out for hours into
the black and jagged night.

for years now, he's been out playing
the larger boys falling on him
like supple oaks.

when he comes inside
his thousand cowlicks stand up
he's my porcupine
he smells strongly
of the earth, wind.

three years ago,
he pledged his devotion
and what if his wife objected?
I asked,
"I'd kick her out," he said
and I can see the maneuver
fast, military, clean.

he's all boy
I must approach circle him
a pilot
scanning searching scanning for
fewer and smaller
and finally microscopic openings.

Birth

Gravitationally bound
down chute
the form ploughs
         round bone warrens
pounding hard
driving down,
a cudgel,
this soon-to-be child
becoming a hurricane force
upon barrier island

then stops
jerks
re-starts,
a train with errant brakes.

Contraction comes.
"Now. Push. Push hard now,"
the nurse intones.
Her strength sapped,
depleted, my daughter struggles
cannot summon up requisite force,
her pain, now diffuse, sharp.
The form slides up,
a guerilla army after a rout.

And who could blame it?
Perhaps it thinks,
why go
from pupa—
puerperal warmth,
substrate of loam,

membranous light
skeins of muscle
to enter roiling world
or does it think at all?

Doctor casts worried eye
at the monitor,
its peaks now troughs,
summons a colleague
who nods,
agrees the head's position is odd.

"You can do this!
Push hard
it's almost out!"
a voice
pleads loud,
mine.
"You don't have to shout,"
the doctor chides.
But I do.
I know my only daughter
fledged her,
my youngest
who, like this child
resisted coming forth.

Yellow appears
at aperture
hair or lanugo.
"I see the head.
One more push and
it's out!" I cry.

Crowning, they call it,
as in royal.
Child is displayed
held aloft
with magisterial flourish.

Afterbirth
is tugged,
lugged out,
an afterthought.
It falls to the floor,
a color chart:
barn red,
gentian,
mustard yellow,
forming eddies.

This beauteous child
arms unfurled,
surveys all
with eyes primitive
wizened.

Dad

1.

In mirrored showrooms
swatches hung from
your broad fingers
lace:
Venise, Alençon
redolent of royalty
of foreign places
claret
night-navy
the season's colors.
Between 36th Street and 40th
Broadway and Eighth Avenues
you were known,

2.

you went door to door
office to office
paper grit swirling
subway spuming below
"Jack," you'd say
to a man like yourself
small, barrel-chested
"you remember my daughter
the middle one?"

3.

and Jack would smile
and say how pretty I was and
how big I'd grown.
In high-ceilinged warehouses
we'd walk down aisles
clogged with women's blouses
past dark eyed women sewing
who'd look up
and smile.

4.

You were seventy five
and still, the first one
on the train every day,
sometimes in darkness
battered attache case
beside you.
"Don't worry, I'll get you
the goods,"
you promised the buyers
and you did, Dad,

5.

lace salesman, provider
but it was getting harder.
"Nat, I can't see you now,"
a much younger man said,

your presence an impertinence,
"the young bucks,"
I think you called them
sons of business owners mostly.

6.

Pushed out by the man
you brought in
treated like a son
you saw your end,
craved it.
Death hung nearby
heavy curtain upon a scanty rod.

7.

Now retired, you visited
gardens mansions.
Standing behind velvet ropes
we heard stories
of captain of industries
their wives and average sons.
You liked that.
Still other days we drove around,
the world pink,
magnolias, thick with buds.
In a museum I posed you
under Red Grooms canvas
bristling alive
under stars.

8.

Your last year was hard.
Something had bored into
your core
saw you quietly reeling
your stride
now a shamble
shoulders,
a universal shrug.
Oh Poppa why couldn't I see
you were not given to
observation of the natural world
(although each Spring
you heralded
the arrival of the robins
"Amazing, you'd say,
"How they always know
to come.")
You drifted through shopping malls
anonymous
the mind still incisive.

9.

You had been in
the Intensive Care Unit
many times
always the least sick
your heartbeat irregular, slow
and I'd say, "at least you don't
look like them"

the alone insensate ones
and you'd ask, "Did you
write the speech yet?"
It was our joke
our soft shoe
and I told you,
"nope."

10.

But now it was time.
In the Emergency Room
I saw a small tic
pulse in your cheek
where it hadn't pulsed
for a generation
and, as the hours charged
into muzzy night,
dawn greeted me,
an indiscriminate halloo,
your tongue now
hard thick black
a parrot's, eyes
once cerulean now
a moonless Atlantic.
Oh, inchoate world
of my ancient silent keening!

11.

Sometimes I hear you
not the voice, though
"never drive so fast
you can't stop if a
child ran into the street,"
or did you mean my life?
You stopped at a red light.
Your heart stopped.
You went door to door
office to office,
your world was small
and I have grown smaller
as the world has, alone.

My Favorite Photograph

In puffy winter coats
hardy, no hats
my three children
spun in oversized playground pot
lying down
bodies, lined up
pistons
When asked
they dragged their feet, stopped,
shoes stuttering on asphalt
smiled for the camera
young enough to want
to please.

Disquieted by those repetitions
playing in my limbic system
in low gear,
I felt my world
was pinhole small.

They didn't know
I was thinking,
it takes a long time
to raise a child,
wondered how time
would pass,
whether at trot or amble,
asked myself
how I would get through it.
Did.

She Started to Find Herself in Strange Cities

She does not think
she will go crazy
or be expected to.
She'd have known.
Her mind,
even at its worst,
was a controlled forest fire.

Still
she worries over
small things
forgotten bills or
that this poem
created on phone
might dissipate like some
childhood toy,
magnetic shavings
hanging from
a grinning man's face,

or that Botero's
bland blank
large hipped sculptures
she saw today
in the Time Warner building
have landed in this poem.

On Mom's Yahrzeit, on the Second Anniversary of Her Death

That first year
I'd forget.
I'd start to call you.

Your home of fifty-six years
my childhood home, is
ploughed up,
stand of elephant-legged
hundred-year old beech trees,
undulant land I sledded on,
leveled, sheared.

Today,
the anniversary of your death,
I find a note I wrote,
"Get Mom support stockings."
I feel a jolt.

I wear your sweater,
navy, white polka dots
one of the few you
bought for yourself.
A motherless child, you were
uneasy with others' kindness
even mine, asking if I'd mind
fetching you a glass of water.

Mom:
I'm remembering your hands,
soft, cats' ears,
folding back my cuffs

with smart flick of wrist
as I fold my granddaughter's blouse
although my gesture's not as crisp.

Subway Poses

When he looks egret-eyed steady,
fingers bent,
a crab's claw
draped across his face,
an exotic curtain of beads
that clink when parted,
enlarged eye
beneath glasses,
feral,
he looks pitiable,
a Poe character.

A man with a suitcase
looks pained
shifts his weight.
Hope plays upon his parted lips
as if catching spring rain
or dew's descent.

Feet athwart,
a Peter Lorre look-alike
plants himself athwart the door.
An exaggerated specimen
of adult male *Homo sapien*
he's a sideshow attraction:
the muscleman,
the only thing missing:
a handlebar mustache.

Man with two kids,
boys, hair braided,
school-aged,
sleeps,

extra fold of skin
beneath his chin, a
weariness, a giving in.
He wakes, listens, grins.
He dotes on his kids.
They still care.

One man's long lean fingers
resemble Horowitz's.
Lacing them together,
he forms a nest. Frowns.

Some guy is whistling
while listening to music.
He doesn't know he's audible
which isn't a crime
unlike expectorating
on my shoe
which someone almost did.

Man rages, lurches,
spins,
a top unmoored.
All heads bow
as he departs,
then stumbles back,
recites an imprecation.

A woman cradles a book,
her prize,
another woman,
her child.

Nights, I hear
Long Island Railroad train's horn,
a bleat a lowing
a lung expelling
sustained note
the kind Walt Whitman would have sung
had he stayed
on the North Shore
of Long Island
where I lived most of my life
where he was born
walked upon hills large, fecund,
where we both walked, on Jayne's Hill,
Long Island's highest point.

Lissa, 1969 and 1970, Summers

Her body squat, solid, thick,
Lissa leaned heavily upon me,
flute thin,
a listing ship
both of us, seventeen.
Taller by a head
I steered her down
steep hills
cobbled streets
to local doctor
translating English to Spanish
Spanish to English.
Recovering quickly,
she was blithe about her near-
        miss,
she'd forgotten to
inject her insulin.

The locals:
servants scurrying
to early morning mass at
Church of the Nuns,
its spire high enough to
pierce a cloud,
Raimundo, an American,
who said he'd performed
on the streets of Chicago,
guerrilla theater,
and why doubt him,
who everyone thought was
a narc but smoked with him
and Jan, who,

even with that scar
running halfway down her face
was beautiful so you'd notice,
who I badly wished I could ask,
how?

Memory lifts, a scrim:
Lissa, from the Los Angeles Valley
before Valley Girl was a thing,
and I, from the East Coast,
went out each night
to the discotheque, *La Fragua,*
she to watch her American
boyfriend rock band leader,
his gnarled body
a vine snaking up a banyan;
me,
to watch my boyfriend sort-of,
Fernando the drummer.

We had little in common
than the apartment we shared
and my favorite Superman
tee shirt which disappeared.

The following summer
we shared an apartment in Los Angeles.
We made rubber stamps,
the glue, pungent
redolent of commerce.
Stamps trumpeting
in double legged letters

Net 10/30
High priority.
Fans whirred
fanning our
productivity.

A dry hot LA summer
superior to torpid
New York ones
the locals said.
Hellacious hot.

Lissa and I lost touch.
For years I pined for
my lost Superman shirt.

But this past summer
I thought of her,
googled her, summoned her
memory up,
Dead at twenty-eight.

Leavetaking, A Guide

When thrust out of,
rousted from
billowy somnolence,
while nuzzled
nosed into
by heat-seeking missile
while asleep,
their protestations ignored
all demurrals having failed,
some women do what they feel
they must
and give in.

Once goaded,
compliant docile bulls,
they remain silent
except for maybe
a snort or two
which may just be breathing.
The getting-over-with is
a mechanical street sweeping
but not painless nor clean.

A man may,
if so inclined,
praise her, tell her she is good or
that she has improved,
may think she likes hearing
this.

The act is anodyne to him.
Were there to be a phrase
it might be
sleep interruptus

which deserves a hashtag
or subreddit
or perhaps is.

A question:
should developing a technique
to shorten the duration
be regarded
as small victory?

When a woman decides
she will no longer
drop anchor
he may accuse her of
perpetrating a scam, grift,
even after half a lifetime of
shared bed, children
other connubial duties
at which point
evacuation must be stealthy,
swift
and preferably
aided by others
the safest place,
Mother's.

And there is a
conclusiveness
to being alive
to tell the story
with steady beat
of heart.

Male Cardinals

Dee-dooo. Dee-dooo.
Repeatedly. Unrelenting.
Poor dears.   All they want is a piece of   the action.
Their dilemma: a slimming out of prospects. For a reason.
Tell them, these bachelor birds.
Perhaps it will help.
Perhaps then they will be silent
or will bring it down a notch.   Male Cardinals: the cold callers
of   the avian kingdom.

Supermarket

When I was younger
cashiers gave my babies bananas.
I took them.
Our eyes met.
We smiled,
complicit.
I wanted to break out in song
in the frozen food aisle.

But still I wondered why.
We were not poor
the children not undernourished,
bathed.
The girl, in cowboy shirt
with brother's name embossed upon it
the younger boy
all cowlicks, raffish in his
Oshkosh B'Gosh overalls,
the oldest, somber, wearing Carter's,
and all three for the most part
presentable, I thought.

Once, years before,
my son grabbed a Mickey plush toy,
or I gave it to him to amuse him.
When I realized I hadn't paid
we'd already left,
felt no remorse.
Was I a thief,
I wondered,
but not for long.

Now older,
the children grown,
I shop at my corner bodega,
know everyone by name.
Now and again
the cashiers cut me bargains
or throw me the occasional freebie.

Complicit, we smile.